Women to Fly

by Mei Hua Chen

PEARSON
Scott Foresman

Editorial Offices: Glenview, Illinois • Parsippany, New Jersey • New York, New York
Sales Offices: Needham, Massachusetts • Duluth, Georgia • Glenview, Illinois
Coppell, Texas • Sacramento, California • Mesa, Arizona

In 1903, two brothers did something amazing. Wilbur and Orville Wright flew a plane! No one had ever done this before. Soon people all over the world were interested in flight. One of those people was Harriet Quimby.

Harriet was born in Michigan in 1875. In 1910, Harriet attended an air show. People watched airplane flights. She was amazed to see the pilots fly the planes upside down and in circles. She decided to prove that a woman could fly a plane as well as a man. In 1911, she became the first woman in America to get a pilot's license.

Soon Harriet was flying in air shows. She was daring. People loved to watch her do flying tricks.

Harriet Quimby

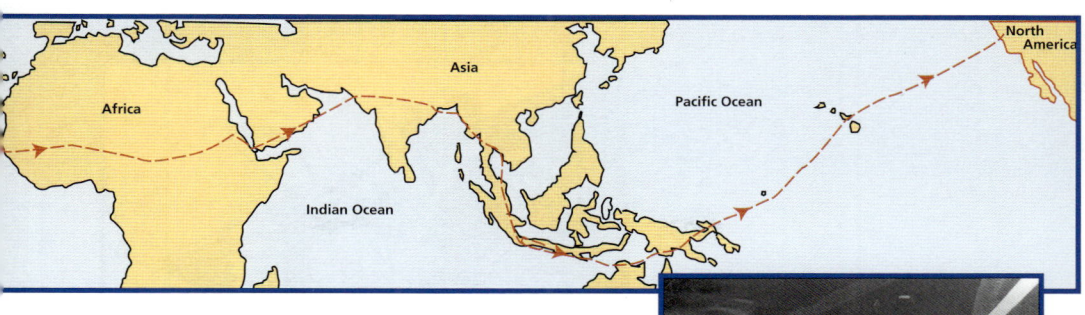

Planned route for Amelia Earhart's flight around the world.

Amelia Earhart is the most famous of all female aviators. Amelia was born in 1897 in Kansas. In 1922, she earned her pilot's license. Amelia set her first flight record that same year. She flew up to 14,000 feet above the ground.

Amelia Earhart

In 1932, Amelia reached another goal. She flew solo across the Atlantic Ocean. It was the first flight across the Atlantic by a woman.

Amelia wanted to be the first person to fly around the world at its widest point. On June 1, 1937, Amelia began this flight in Florida. By July 2, Amelia had flown over 22,000 miles. She had less than 7,000 miles to go. During a storm, Amelia's plane disappeared over the Pacific Ocean. Amelia and her plane were never found.

---

record: better performance than anyone before her

Katherine Cheung was born in China in 1904. At the age of 17, she left her family to come to the United States to study music. Later, her family joined her in Los Angeles.

Chinese women did not drive cars in those days. Katherine's father taught her to drive anyway. Soon she was looking for more excitement. She took flying lessons.

Katherine Cheung

After only twelve and a half hours of training, her teacher let her fly solo. In 1932, she became the first Asian American woman to earn a pilot's license.

Katherine flew in air races and quickly became a popular star in air shows.

Jackie Cochran

Jackie Cochran was born sometime before 1913. As a young woman, Jackie became interested in flying and got a pilot's license.

Jackie is best known for her contribution during World War II. She thought that, if women could fly army planes, then more soldiers could concentrate on fighting. In 1940, she wrote to the president's wife, Eleanor Roosevelt. She suggested that the country let women fly for the Air Force. Thanks to Jackie's hard work, a women's branch of the Air Force was formed during World War II. In 1943, Jackie was asked to lead the Women's Air Force Service Pilots, or WASPs.

Eileen Collins

Eileen Collins represents the spirit of all women who dared to fly. From a very young age, Eileen dreamed of flying a Space Shuttle.

To make her dream come true, Eileen studied math, science, and space systems. In July of 1991, Eileen became an astronaut. Then, in 1995, she became the first female Space Shuttle pilot.

In July of 1999, NASA chose Eileen Collins to be the first woman to command a Space Shuttle. After the announcement, Eileen said, "It is my hope that all children—boys and girls—will see this mission and be inspired to reach for their dreams, because dreams do come true."

NASA: the National Aeronautics and Space Administration; the United States space program

mission: trip with a goal or a job to do

Kalpana Chawla was born in India in 1961. In 1994, she was chosen as an astronaut by NASA. She worked on computers in the spacecraft.

Kalpana Chawla

Kalpana's second NASA flight was on Space Shuttle *Columbia* in January of 2003. On this research mission, Kalpana and the rest of the team did many experiments.

The mission ended in tragedy. Space Shuttle *Columbia* was returning to Earth at the end of the mission when it broke apart over Texas. All seven astronauts were killed.

1903	Orville and Wilbur Wright fly a plane.
1911	Harriet Quimby becomes the first woman pilot.
1932	Amelia Earhart is the first woman to fly solo across the Atlantic Ocean.
	Katherine Cheung becomes the first female Asian American pilot.
1937	Earhart disappears over the Pacific Ocean during a worldwide flight.
1943	Jackie Cochran leads the WASPs during World War II.
1995	Eileen Collins becomes first female Space Shuttle pilot.
1999	Eileen Collins becomes the first female commander of a Space Shuttle.
2003	Kalpana Chawla flies as an astronaut on Space Shuttle *Columbia*.